A LifeWay Ministry

TRUE LOVE WAITS

Takes a Look at
Courting, Dating, & Hanging Out

The Guys' Book

David Payne
With Raymond and Hannah Vogtner,
Kristi Cherry, Tracey Bumpus,
and Matt Tullos

LifeWay Press®
Nashville, Tennessee

ISBN 978-0-6330-0463-7

Item 001114514

Dewey Decimal Classification Number: 306.73

Subject Heading: TEENAGERS / SEXUAL BEHAVIOR / DATING / SOCIAL CUSTOMS

Printed in the United States of America

Student Ministry Publishing
LifeWay Church Resources
One LifeWay Plaza
Nashville, TN 37234-0144

We believe that the Bible has God for its author; salvation for its end; and truth, without any
mixture of error, for its matter and that all Scripture is totally true and trustworthy.
The 2000 statement of *The Baptist Faith and Message* is our doctrinal guideline.

Unless otherwise indicated, Scripture quotations are from
the Holy Bible, New International Version. Copyright © 1973, 1978, 1984
by International Bible Society. Used by permission.

Contents

You da Man!

The Power Is in Your Hands

C'mon! Be a man!" his friends shouted at him. He stood on the edge of the cliff looking down at the pool of water 45 feet below. He felt a tremendous amount of pressure to jump. His manhood was in question. A test had been set before him. A challenge had been issued! He could prove to his buddies that he was a man simply by jumping into the pool below. They would shout, "You da man!" and he would be their hero.

What if he decided not to jump? What if he simply walked away and said, "I'm not really into killing myself today"? How would they respond? Would they reject him? They certainly wouldn't shout, "You da man!" But would his manhood be in question? What difference does it make if it is?

The situations change throughout life. Maybe you aren't being challenged to jump from a 45-foot cliff. Maybe it's a can of beer, or going over the speed limit, or teasing a classmate who is different. Maybe it is the urge to create dating conquests and situations to brag about in the locker room. Every time, you feel like your manhood is in question, or perhaps you feel it needs to be proven. This raises the question, "What does it mean to be a man?"

In three sentences, write your definition of manhood.

_____

_____

_____

_____

_____

_____

What Does It Mean to Be a Man?

Manhood vs. Machismo

Oftentimes, machismo, or an exaggerated sense of masculine pride, replaces manhood. According to the dictionary, manhood, simply defined, means the condition of being an adult male. Unfortunately, as each person tries to define _adult male,_ there are some confusing and conflicting messages. Some think being an adult male means not having to stop and ask for directions when you are lost. Others think it means to be able to hold off fits of emotion, particularly when it involves tears.

Machismo is the result of an overdose of testosterone, but we will deal with that in a bit. Many men have gotten in fights and other difficult situations because they had to prove their manhood by being the victor in any given situation. That is not what manhood is all about.

The Hormone Factor

How can you be a man when you are still just a teenager? The answer to that question is that physically and anatomically, you are no different than a guy who is in college.

Hormonal changes start when you are very young and explode in the early teen years. Hormones, in a very sneaky and insidious way, are slowly released into your body, causing differences in the way your body works and in the way your mind thinks. Once these hormones start spilling over into your body, it is something that will happen for the rest of your life. As this continues, you will have to deal with your hormones in an appropriate way.

These hormones can cause some confusing responses at times. They have a strange capacity to turn an otherwise normal and nice young man into a self-absorbed, self-gratifying person with a one-track mind, pleasing self. Unfortunately this usually happens in the area of your sexuality. Your body is changing so quickly that your mind doesn't know exactly how to keep up and often gives in to a good feeling experience rather than learning how to control your newfound maturity.

Read _1 Corinthians 6:19_. The instruction given here is to honor God with your body. This is a blanket statement with no exceptions. It does not say honor God with your body except when your hormones are raging. How can you honor God with your body? List all the possible ways here (not just sexual ones)._____

_____

_____

_____

_____

_____

Alike But Different

You, as a male, are different than the female of your species. Duh! It is truly an obvious statement, but when males interact with females and females interact with males, in some ways they expect the other gender to think the same way as they do. So, the obvious reminder remains. You are different!

The physical differences are obvious, but males and females are also alike. They are both created in the image of God *(Gen. 1:27)*, and their basic physical forms are somewhat similar. The social differences, however, are more pronounced.

When men talk, what do they most often talk about? List as many different types of topics as you can think of. _____

_____

_____

_____

How We Are Wired

Males are aroused by visual stimulation more than women. That's why there is more pornographic smut directed at you than at her. The powerful images are addictive and very hard to erase.

We daydream or think about sex more than girls do. Don't feel like you are a horrible person if you think about sex. However, a preoccupation with sex and the girls you are around may lead you into compromise. Constantly entertaining these thoughts will eventually cause you to look at women simply as sex objects rather than children of God. Most girls would be totally shocked by how strong an impulse males have.

Here are a few tips if you feel that you are struggling with the power of your sex drive and are tired of taking a cold shower every other hour:

1. Find two or three other guys and develop an accountability agreement. Having a strong sex drive is not something to feel shame about. Meet and pray together. Take the first step. I'm sure that the other guys will be glad you did!

2. Don't feed the fire with sexually explicit fuel: MTV, pornography,

other forms of trash media. Don't trust yourself with unfiltered internet access.

3. Don't buy into the lie that long, deep kissing and other sexually stimulating activities with a girl will curb your appetite for sex. It does not work that way. You'll end up compromising your values and hers and you'll end up wanting more and more until finally you reach orgasm. After this you experience a flood of guilt, the likes of which you have never experienced. It's not fulfilling, and you could permanently corrupt your sexual identity and self-image.

4. Don't condemn yourself for having a sex drive. Sex is a beautiful gift that is reserved for marriage. Unfortunately, you received the drive to express that gift several years before you would normally marry. So avoid the traps mentioned earlier and don't spend time raking yourself through the coals about having passing thoughts about sex.

List any other ideas that have worked for you in your attempt to preserve your manhood and sexual integrity.

_____

_____

_____

_____

_____

_____

_____

_____

Top 10 Lies & Cop-outs

Avoiding Head-on Collisions

After an extensive survey of students, youth pastors, parents, teachers, and hot dog vendors, we proudly present: The Top Ten Lies and Cop-outs of Courting and Dating—from the home office in Sioux City, Iowa.

The List

10. MTV, Hollywood, and secular magazines provide a good basis for getting a healthy understanding of dating and sex.

Most guys spend more time in front of the tube than they do passionately seeking God for lifestyle choices.

What are some of the messages that the media transmits about girls? _____

_____

_____

_____

Movies and magazines use everything from camera tricks to enticing dialogue to keep your mind focused on the wrong messages. The more you turn your attention to what they are pitching, the more you begin to think you are missing out. Their false worldview teaches that all you have to do is buy a product or drive a new car and you'll receive everything in this cultural fantasy world, including sexual fulfillment. Nothing could be farther from the truth. The enticements of the media are intoxicating, but they are also toxic.

9. Girls are more interested in how you look than in your ability to be self-controlled.

This is all another part of the cultural conspiracy. The media wants to sell you the idea that good looks and a great body are the main attraction for women. In reality, trust and self-control are viewed by most girls as an even greater draw. This doesn't apply to every female, but be careful when you find a girl that makes a bigger deal about physical looks than trust and self-control. Those are the girls you want to run away from as fast as you can! One day your looks will fade. The body is temporal, but the spirit is eternal. The guy who places his mindset on this earth suit will ultimately lose. Self-control and trust are traits that will ultimately determine your destiny.

What we are talking about here is a hunger for wisdom that totally dominates all of your urges. It guides your path. A righteous man grabs hold of the steering wheel and chooses the right path. That path is not only godly but also very attractive to girls.

My son, pay attention to what I say; listen closely to my words.
Do not let them out of your sight; keep them within your heart;
For they are life to those who find them and health to a man's whole body.
Above all else, guard your heart, for it is the wellspring of life.
Proverbs 4:20-23

According to this Scripture, how does a guy truly become righteous? _____

_____

_____

"I am attracted to a guy who doesn't spend a ton of time trying to be cool and wanting to look great. I'm looking for a guy who treats me like a person and not a prize. I want him to take the lead, to know how to say 'no' to compromise."

Marci R.
Bridgeport, Connecticut

8. I can have sex with a girl and still have a good premarital relationship with her.

This is the type of thing we see portrayed on TV every other minute. A couple has sex, and then they decide to just be friends and everything works out fine. They are still close friends, and they still hang out together. It's the "No harm, no foul rule." Yeah right...It is a lie! When you have sex with someone, the relationship is forever changed. There's no going back.

Think of all the changes:
• A sexual relationship tears down just about every boundary of the relationship. It strips away the intimate details of your body, your senses, and your mind. The experiences cannot be erased from your mind. You will never look at that girl in the same way as you looked at her before you had the sexual encounter.
• When you get married, you will compare the sexual experience with the girlfriend to the relationship with your wife. You'll also realize that you trashed a gift that was rightfully your wife's to be given to her on your wedding night.
• If the relationship dissolves (which happens 98 percent of the time), it will multiply the pain of the break-up. Once you walk out of a relationship entangled in sex, there is no exit without a bombardment of hurt, shame, regret, and fear.

Can you think of other ways sex can damage a relationship?

_____

_____

_____

_____

_____

7. A good way to satisfy sexual urges is by feeding your mind pornography.

This is a strange lie that a surprising number of guys believe. But as time passes, the person who buys into this will come to realize that he was duped at a very high price.

One of the ways that guys differ from girls is that we are wired differently. As you probably already know (if you are a guy), we are easily aroused by sight. Seeing graphic sexual images can be so powerful that after you see the image, in truth, you never lose it. It has been burned into the hard drive of your brain, and this is one file that can't be deleted.

When a guy looks at pornography, a chemical reaction happens in the brain that can make pornography just as addictive as crack cocaine. Breaking its grip on you can be maddening.

Another lie about pornography is that it is a victimless crime. The guy who views porn will be scarred. It will weaken his future marriage. Many high school and college guys believe that pornography can be a temporary fix until they get married. That's not true either. You will discover that the lure of pornography lingers even after marriage. And sometimes its power becomes even stronger, hurling you into even deeper bondage.

Pornography is also a progressive trap. A guy might start out looking at the *Sports Illustrated Swimsuit Issue* or watching a PG-13 movie love scene. Sooner or later, those things will not give him a rush like they did at first; so he'll search for images, sounds, and experiences that are a little more graphic. After a while the guy will find himself farther and farther down the road into hard-core pornography. Then the guy's compulsive behavior of masturbating with pornography is no longer controlled by him. He is now being controlled by the pornography. Count on it—the more fuel you pour on a lust problem, the more the fire will consume your mind.

Although the end result is different from person to person, it has to be noted that almost every serial murderer and sex offender began their journey to the depths of their depraved behavior with pornography. Pornography is sham and a chief tool of Satan in the 21st century. Don't trust yourselves, guys. Stay away from pay-per-view opportunities and bookstores that sell porn. Avoid unfiltered internet access. Even the availability is not worth the risk.

Porn is also a crime against your future wife. The husband will enter the marriage with a view of sexuality that is tainted, twisted, and just plain wrong. Ultimately the wife pays a price for the choices of her husband.

Read Matthew 5:27-38. How does this verse apply to porn?

_____

_____

_____

_____

The Good News
If you've dabbled in pornography, things are not as hopeless as they may seem, because God promises victory over temptation. The Bible says, *"No temptation has seized you except what is common to man. And*

God is faithful; he will not let you be tempted beyond what you can bear. But when you are tempted, he will also provide a way out so that you can stand up under it" (1 Corinthians 10:13).

However, it is important that we do our part by avoiding the places and things which trigger lust and by focusing our mind on Christ and things that are wholesome (Colossians 3:1-4; Philippians 4:8).

6. I'm not a man until I have sex.

It doesn't take a big man to have sex. It takes a real man to say no to sex. And the time to say no is not when you are faced with a compromising situation. Decide now that you will make the True Love Waits commitment. Keep your commitment in sight. Talk about it with the guys you are around. The more you verbalize the commitment, the more it will become a part of you.

Whenever you accepted Christ as your Savior, you made a commitment to a different lifestyle. The rules changed.

In the space below, write words that communicate how the world's ways can be changed to God's way.

The World's Way	God's Way
self-centered	Christ-centered
impatient	_____
easily angered	_____
motivated by lust	_____

Now look at the chart on the next page. Think about statements that would describe God's Way as opposed to The World's Way, and complete the chart with those statements.

The World's Way	God's Way
• Does anything to get a girl to compromise.	• Honors a girl by showing virtue and integrity.
• Keeps a list of sexual conquests.	•
• Acts sly and preys on a girl's weakness.	•
• Always on the hunt for a new thrill.	•

5. I can keep my commitment to virginity by doing everything but intercourse.

Here's another weird and illogical statement about sex before marriage. Sadly enough, many are fooled into this belief system. Christians seem to want to rank sexual activity and say, "We crossed the line, but I'm still a virgin because we didn't have intercourse." The plain truth is that God wants us to be pure. He wants our minds and bodies to be focused on Him.

Paul the Apostle told the Philippians:
Summing it all up. Friends, I'd say you'll do your best by filling your minds and meditating on things true, noble, reputable, authentic, compelling and gracious—the best, not the worst; the beautiful, not the ugly; things to praise not to curse. [1]

4. Having a sexual relationship with a girl I'm dating will increase my satisfaction in the relationship.

On the contrary. Throwing sex into a dating relationship is similar to throwing a hand grenade into a foxhole. Because you'll know you are outside of God's will in the relationship, you'll feel a sense of shame.

What Is the Difference Between Shame and Guilt?

Guilt is a wrongness of action. When we do something wrong we feel a sense of guilt. We should. Guilt is a gift. Sounds strange doesn't it? But the Holy Spirit deals with our sin, and we carry the guilt of the sin until we repent of it and confess the sin.

Shame, however, is not from God. Shame is a wrongness of being. It doesn't say, "You've made a mistake." It says, "You *are* a mistake!" So how does shame work within the life of the Christian? Satan uses shame to condemn us and to paralyze us. We begin to feel incapable of being used by God. We feel unable to minister or to worship God. Satan, the accuser, reminds us of our sin and heaps a feeling of wrongness upon us. The message we receive is that we can't change and that we are beyond help.

So what does this have to do with sexual activity before marriage? Satan uses our sin to shame us away from God's throne. We feel alone. Like Adam and Eve, we hide from God because we feel ashamed.

When we feel a sense of shame, it is impossible to have a functional relationship. As Christians we will feel a sense of condemnation and we will build walls of defiance not only toward God but also toward the sex partner. Satisfaction is never the real end result of a sexual relationship outside of marriage. It may seem fulfilling at first; but the feeling won't stick around long, and the person that you wanted to share everything with not long ago will be the person you want to run away from.

3. Because you pick up the tab you should expect something from your date.

There is one word that briefly describes this concept: prostitution.

Whenever you feel like you have the right for sexual arousal because you shelled out a few bucks, you've turned the date into an undercover brothel or escort service. Don't even go there. Set the standard higher, and you'll be glad you did.

2. Dating is the best way to get to meet girls.

If you've been on a date, describe what you did to prepare for that very first date: _____

_____

_____

_____

_____

_____

_____

Chances are you spent a great deal of time primping and preparing. If you are like most, you prayed for a clear complexion and a good-hair day. The dating ritual is like a dance of deception. We dress up, smell good, and downplay every negative emotion or physical feature. Therefore, it could be said that the dating scene is a lousy set-up for intimacy and self-disclosure. It's just not how the game is played in most situations. The best place to meet girls is where the focus is not on the relationship but on a common effort and goal.

The best relationships rarely start at the front door of the girl's house. Rather, they begin on a ministry assignment, a school project, or a church mission trip. In these arenas where the accent is on working together, you can find out how girls operate and react to real-world situations. Do they have a good sense of humor? How do they handle conflict? How do they handle money? These are the issues that matter infinitely more than the color of their hair or their taste in clothes.

Write some characteristics you are looking for in a girl.

_____
_____
_____
_____
_____

Begin praying today that God, in His own way and in His own time, will begin preparing you for His plan for you.
And the number one lie and cop-out on romance and relationships is… (Drum roll please.)

1. Be careful about asking God to direct you to your mate. You'll end up spending your life with a boring wife that you didn't want in the first place.

Wrong! So wrong! If you commit your future marriage to the Lord and wait on God, He will blow you away when you finally meet the girl He has chosen for you.

Write your name in the blanks below:

_"For I know the plans I have for _____, declares the Lord, plans to prosper _____ and not to harm you, plans to give _____ hope and a future."_
(Jeremiah 29:11)

If you commit to believing what God says about you and your future, begin to accept God's truth and reject these lies and cop-outs.

------

1. Eugene H. Peterson, _The Message_ (Colorado Springs: NavPress, 1995).

Getting Started in Dating or Courting

Getting Your Signals Straight

In this session we'll take a look at the definitions of dating and courting and also see how both of these strategies begin. As you read the material and work through these issues, begin to pray that God will give you courage and an open mind to choose courting, dating, or hanging out. Let's go!

Is dating just a social outing? A casual acquaintance? What is it? It would be easy to quickly adopt a bad definition of dating. What is your definition of dating? _____

_____

_____

_____

_____

_____

_____

_____

Dating is a relatively new cultural concept, and it has changed drastically from its early days until now.

Which one of the following opinions sounds like you?

❏ Dating is such a sham! It's all so fake. Once you go out with someone, it's like you are making a statement to that person that you are wanting to get all wrapped up emotionally with her. Gag! Who needs that?

❏ Dating is fun. I love the way it makes me feel when I'm getting to know a girl. First kisses are the best. I don't like to lead girls on; but I do enjoy the chase, if you know what I mean. So do I think about dating as a prelude to marriage? No way.

❏ Dating is another word for time bomb. It will end up in a ton of hurt feelings and moral compromise. I want to find a mate in the next 10 years, but dating is not the way I want to find her. I know that God will show me who I should marry. But if you are waiting for me to call, don't hold your breath.

So you don't like any of those? Write your own. _____
_____
_____

Let's think about the following statements. Do they ring true? Answer yes or no.

1. Dating almost always ends up in heartbreak. _____

2. Dating is a good way to lose your standards and maybe even your virginity. _____

3. Most of my friends date just to have fun. No one takes it seriously. It's just a warm-up for the day when we'll really be looking for a mate. _____

The Dating Destination

As you start dating, there are many challenges along the way. Before you ever begin dating someone, it is important to ask: Where is this relationship heading? If we continue to date, what is our destination?

As a man, it is important that you have a destination in mind before you become entangled in the romance that so often accompanies dating. Start thinking this direction by answering the following question.

What is the goal of a dating relationship? _____

_____

_____

_____

For many, the goals are to have fun, to socialize, and to try and find the right person to marry.

The Dating Treasure Map!

Use the space below to draw a sort of treasure map. Start where you think you are right now and draw a map that includes the destinations you would like to visit during your dating life. Include destinations such as friendship, laughter, honest sharing, serving, intimacy, etc. Map out the path you would like your dating relationships to take.

The Dating Alternative

Jason and Katie had an interesting relationship. Their friends just couldn't quite figure it out. They did a lot of things together, but it always seemed to be with large groups of people or with their parents. No one ever recalled seeing them together alone, but all were under the impression that they were "exclusive." They had other friends who spent time together; and their relationships were hard to figure out, but it just seemed that they liked to hang out together. Something was different about Jason and Katie, however. Finally, one of their friends grew curious enough to ask Katie about their relationship, and she told them that they were courting. Her friend acted like she knew what she was talking about but really had no clue.

So What's Courtship?

Let's get a dictionary definition first and then work from there. *Webster's Ninth* defines the act of courting as, "to seek to gain or achieve, to seek the affections of, to seek to win a pledge of marriage from, to engage in social activities leading to engagement and marriage."[1]

Courtship is about open and honest exploration of each other's lives and families leading up to engagement and marriage. Courtship is about marriage—you court in order to see if you can be good friends with the person and to see if this is the person you can make a marriage commitment to. There is no romantic interaction until after the commitment to marriage.

Some parents and teens have become disappointed with the dating scene and the pain associated with feeling used in a relationship without commitment. An alternative is gaining popularity among some families. It's actually been around long before Romeo and Juliet were sneaking around trying to get a priest to marry them secretly.

Courtship is almost as old as the Bible! So what is courtship? Circle the best answer.
A. Finding a mate through a rigorous test of skills in the areas of Ping-Pong, ski boarding, and sailing.
B. Laws preventing mutiny of seafaring vessels.
C. A valid alternative to dating that avoids many of the traps, snags, and heartaches that are hard to avoid in the dating process.

If you chose C, you're on the right track. If you didn't, you may have fallen asleep as you were reading and had one of those weird pizza dreams. Before we dive into all this, let's clear up a few misconceptions. Courtship is becoming more and more mainstream. You don't have to be a member of some strange religious sect. People who court rarely end up with a long beard, wearing a black Amish hat. Also, courtship doesn't mean you must marry the person you begin courting. Courtship is a process of strong integrity, which says, "I take my future marriage seriously, and I won't open myself up to all the potential land mines I'm seeing in the dating process."

Here's a short description of the courtship model:
Boy meets girl. That's the way dating starts as well. But it will get different fast. (As in the next step...)

Instead of boy calls girl or girl calls boy, boy calls girl's parents. (Whoa! What a wild concept!) He sets up a meeting with the girl's parents to introduce himself to them while expressing his interest in spending time with their daughter. After this initial meeting, the parents talk with their daughter about this boy, and they share any concerns or observations they have. After that, if all parties are in agreement, the family finds ways to get the two together in appropriate and supervised settings with the express purpose of getting to know each other better.

Describing Courtship
Write some descriptive phrases about courtship.

_____

_____

_____

_____

_____

Not many people understand the whole idea of courtship. In fact, if you took the time to do some simple research you would find varying views on courtship. To some it is a romantic relationship that your parents approve of and are heavily involved in. Some say you should never touch your partner in a courting relationship—no hand holding, no putting your arm around her (even if you are just stretching), and no kissing. Others say that all time spent together is done so in groups. The couple is never alone. Many times they are out with one or both of their parents. One of the hopes is that this would be the only romantic relationship a person has before marriage, though that may not happen in some instances.

Is Courtship for You?
In a nutshell, the emphasis in courtship is to develop a close friendship in order to get to know each other well enough to see if you want to spend the rest of your life with the person. Marriage is the eventual goal of courtship, just as it is in dating. Still courtship is a hard concept for some to consider.

Are you willing to consider courtship as a possible path toward marriage? _____

If not, what frightens you most about courtship? _____

_____

_____

_____

Use the space below to write down what it would take to get you to consider courtship as a viable option to dating and hanging out. _____

_____

_____

A Guy's Start-up Checklist

(Clarification: This is for you only. It is not recommended that you have a girl fill this out herself!)

❑ **The Heart Check:** What is her relationship with the Lord? Have you heard how she became a Christian? Does she share her faith? Is church a social thing, or does she have a passion for God?

❑ **The Sight Check:** Are you attracted to her simply because she stimulates you visually? Does she dress modestly? Does she dress in a way that would lead you to lust?

❑ **The Needs Check:** Do you want to date her because she needs you? A lot of guys find themselves in a relationship because the girl is emotionally wounded. This might be a good motive to be a friend to a girl, but it's a bad place to start a dating relationship.

❑ **Emotional Check:** Does she express her emotions in a healthy way? Is she easily depressed? Is she controlled by her emotions? The secret to successful emotional well-being is being able to express emotions in a Christlike manner.

❑ **The Words Check:** What words or thoughts dominate her conversation? Is she a gossip? Does she speak the best of people, or does she use her words as weapons?

❑ **Home Check:** What kind of relationship does she have with her father and mother? Does she show them respect? If she has brothers or sisters, how does she treat them?

❑ **Money Check:** What emphasis does she place on money? Do new cars, jewelry, and brand name clothes easily impress her?

❑ **Preoccupation Check:** What preoccupies her? Does she feel uncomfortable going out without looking perfect?

Remember: Dating or courting should never be used to attempt to change a person. It's just too emotionally expensive and risky.

Hangin' Out & Havin' Fun! A Really Cool Option...

For many teenagers, their relationship with the opposite sex defies definition. If a guy and a girl go and do something together, it could be as friends or as acquaintances and may have no romantic overtones to it at all. The only description that even comes close is that they hang out together. Is hanging out different than courting? Is it different than dating? In some ways they are different, and in some ways they are the same.

To start with just hanging out and end up involved in a committed romantic relationship is a long journey. When you reach the end, however, it seems to have snuck up on you. You suddenly find yourself romantically attracted to a good friend. It's strange but true; this really happens!

Here are the big three reasons to consider hanging out as a viable alternative to heavy-duty dating.

• When you are with a group of committed friends you are less likely to be drawn into sexual temptation.

• Hanging with friends takes the pressure off of you. You don't have to be Mr. Entertainment for the evening.

• No strings attached. When you go out with a group you can get to know a girl without a ton of pressure.

What are some other benefits of hanging out? _____

_____

_____

_____

_____

_____

Beware!
If you're going to hang out with a group, make sure you hang around with the right group.

Many students make the mistake of hanging out with a crowd of their peers who are minimally committed to purity at best. Then when Friday night rolls around, they go to a party and find out that the crowd that seemed to be students of integrity were simply saving up their wild streaks for the weekend.

"One of the worst experiences I had last year was when I met some guys and girls at church who also happened to go to my school. I enjoyed being around them. Granted, they weren't exactly spiritual leaders in the youth group, but they were really nice. I really liked one of the girls, and she invited me to go to a party with them. So I went and had a great time until I started making some choices I never thought I'd make. Maybe it was the girl that I liked, or maybe it was just that I didn't want them to think I was a dork. For whatever reason, I ended up getting totally wasted for the first

time in my life. I felt horrible the next morning. But even more than the physical drain, I felt like I had spiritually trashed everything I stood for as a committed Christian."

Harold Morris, a well-known Christian writer who spent years inside the South Carolina State Penitentiary, simply stated it this way. "The friends you hang out with in many cases determine the direction of your life."[2]

Believe it. Corrupt or ungodly companions who try to fit you into their mold are dangerously controlling.

Do not be misled: "Bad company corrupts good character."
1 Corinthians 15:33

---

1. *Webster's Collegiate Dictionary,* 9th ed., s.v. "courtship."
2. Harold Morris, *Twice Pardoned* (Arcadia, California: Focus on the Family, 1986).

Guidelines & Pitfalls

Getting Your Mind in Gear

I n this chapter we'll discuss some things that will be crucial if you choose to be righteous while courting, dating, or just hanging out.

Finding the Right Person–
Being the Right Person

In today's society, many people are more focused on finding the right person than on being the right person God wants them to be. You perhaps remember those silly love songs that only forty-year-olds can tolerate.

Ooo-ooo, baby. My world was empty without your love. You drive me crazy, ooo-ooo baby.

I don't care who you are or what you've done, your tender love is all I need.

You get the idea that half the world is counting on some relationship to fill their lives with contentment. But the Bible clearly states you will never be complete if you are looking anywhere other than to Jesus to meet your needs. And there's no way that you can complete someone else's life if she is missing Jesus. Therefore, take the time to prayerfully look over these guidelines. Some of these guidelines are things that you're probably already doing. If so, give yourself a pat on the back. Some of these guidelines may seem a little radical and extreme. Purity in today's culture is an extreme concept, and sometimes the only way you'll be able to guarantee success is to take extreme measures.

Tip #1: Meet the parents of the girl you wish to date before you ask the girl out.

Tip #2: Avoid dark solitary places when you are with a girl.

Read *Ephesians 5:11*.
Why are dark places a danger zone for dating? _____
_____
_____
_____
_____

Tip #3: Develop a prayer relationship with a girl before you develop a dating relationship. If you are united together against the temptation, it's much easier than if you try to manage all the self-control by yourself. Some people are tempted and, like Jesus, they say, "Get thee behind me Satan!" A prayerless Christian might be more prone to say, "Get thee behind me Satan, and push!"

Tip #4: Just say no to "missionary dating." So what's missionary dating? A missionary date is when a Christian goes out with a non-Christian in the hopes of being a witness to the person. The courting or dating arena is not the place to begin an evangelistic emphasis.

Tip #5: Find a girl who is as committed to Jesus as you are. Answer this question: How does she view church? Is church a passionate pursuit of God for her? Or is it just an excuse to see her friends? Here are a few subquestions for this category:

• Does she pray?
• Does she take notes during sermons or Bible studies?
• Does she keep a journal?
• Does she have a passion for Christian music? Praise and worship music?
• Does she volunteer to serve in ministry?
• Does she talk about how God is working around her?

If you answered yes to all these questions, you may have discovered a rare find: a righteous girl who is totally sold out to Christ. If you have no interest in dating her, at least have her put you on her prayer list. If you answered "no" to all these questions, don't even think about dating her. This is a relationship that will be more trouble than you need. Run. Run away as fast as you can!

Tip #6: Be polite! Treat her with the respect you would show an honored guest. OK, guys. We need to talk. We've seen how some of you guys treat the girls. It's pathetic. Follow these rules; and if the girl doesn't want to date you, at least you'll be the most polite, cultured guy she's been around in a long, long time.

• Open the door for your date.
• If you are leaving in a vehicle, open her door and then walk around the front of the car. Not behind the car—in front. I know many guys like to use the walk behind the car method, perhaps in order to check their fly one last time. Check your fly before you start the date and walk around the front of the car.
• Let the girl order her meal first.
• Listen to her. Don't dominate conversations.

- Pray before you eat. Speak blessing on her and her family. Mention her parents by name in your prayer.
- Consult with her on her preferences and don't compromise your values by taking her to places or events that compromise her reputation. This includes movies, guys.

Philippians 4:8 is a good measuring stick. Finally, brothers, whatever is true, whatever is noble, whatever is right, whatever is pure, whatever is lovely, whatever is admirable—if anything is excellent or praiseworthy—think about such things.

Tip #7: Before your date, ask Jesus to make His presence known during your time with the girl. Remind yourself, "I am in Christ. I don't go anywhere without Jesus. I am in His hands. I want to honor Him, not dishonor Him."

Tip #8: Verbalize what your standards are to your date. This will put your date at ease. Plus you'll score some major trust points on the front end. Add a few fumbles and awkward stammers here and there, and you might say something like this:

Lisa, it is so cool that we're going out on this date. I need to tell you something that you might not have ever heard from a guy before. (After she faints, try bringing her back into consciousness and continue.) I've made a commitment to purity. You won't have to worry about me trying to take advantage of you physically or trying to manipulate you emotionally. You won't have to worry about whether I'm going to make a move and try to kiss you on the first date. That's not where I'm at, and I just wanted to let you know. I respect you too much to be selfish.

Tip #9: You are a son of God. Act like it! Enough said. For too long, supposedly good, Christian guys have manipulated and seduced girls to meet their own fantasies and drives. Some generation has got to stand up and say, "No more!"

Tip #10: Work together, act together, think together, and worship together. You don't have to go with your basic "Italian restaurant-movie-and-home-by-10:29-or-else" model for dating. As mentioned earlier, dating is really a lousy way to get to know a girl.

Tip #11: Don't be obsessed with finding God's one for you; just serve God and seek to be who God wants you to be. Then God will bring the one to you!

Tip #12: Examine your heart before you start dating. What kind of person does God want you to be? As you think about and answer this question, use the following Scripture references to guide you.

Write the Scripture reference next to the phrase that best summarizes it.
(I Thessalonians 4:3; I Corinthians 6:12; I Corinthians 6:18,19; I Corinthians 8:13; I Corinthians 10:31)

Don't cause others to sin _____

Glorify God _____

Don't be controlled _____

Your body belongs to Christ _____

Be holy and pure _____

These Scriptures teach us about God's principles regarding relationships. They guide us as we determine our own personal moral standards.

Based on these scriptural principles, what kind of moral standards would you set for yourself when dating? _____
_____
_____
_____
_____

The Good, the Bad, and....

In many cases, dating is a thoughtless, automatic act. In this context, it becomes primarily a selfish act. There are some good reasons to date; and, of course, there are also some bad reasons to date. From the reasons listed below, check the appropriate box.

Good ❑ Bad ❑   1. Get to know someone better

Good ❑ Bad ❑   2. Prestige

Good ❑ Bad ❑   3. Spouse seeking

Good ❑ Bad ❑   4. Make someone jealous

Good ❑ Bad ❑   5. Grow socially, emotionally, spiritually

Good ❑ Bad ❑   6. Sex

Good ❑ Bad ❑   7. Fun

Good ❑ Bad ❑   8. Avoid isolation

Good ❑ Bad ❑   9. Learn how to better communicate with the opposite sex

Good ❑ Bad ❑   10. Help fulfill a need to love and be loved

Good ❑ Bad ❑   11. Get a better idea of what we want our future mate to look like

As you look over your markings, I think you will find that all the bad reasons to date involve reducing the other person to a means to a desired end. When trying to think of good reasons to date, try to remember the scriptural principles we studied earlier and combine them with the reasons you would like for a person to be dating you.

It's All About Attitude

Your attitude is the final factor. In *2 Corinthians 5:9*, Paul says, "We *make it our goal to please Him...*" Paul is not talking about dating in this passage. He is, however, talking about living a Christian life. Everything we do should be done to please God. That includes dating.

Write an honest prayer to God indicating your willingness to please Him. _____

_____

_____

_____

_____

_____

_____

_____

_____

Session 5

The Final Destination

Know Where You Are Going

So we've just about finished a cram-session on the concepts, choices, and pitfalls of courting, dating, and hanging out.

How has your view of courting, dating, and hanging out changed since you started this study? _____

_____

_____

_____

Let's wrap up by underscoring a vital truth and putting a major exclamation mark at the end of it. Begin with the end in mind!

Perhaps 80-90 percent of all students who are developing relationships do so without even looking at an overall purpose.

It's similar to eating Rocky Road ice cream. Why do you eat it? Is it to promote proper oral hygiene? Is it because you want to add more fiber to your diet? Is it because you want to add more muscle mass? Unless you've been brainwashed by the sales manager of a local ice cream parlor, your answer to all of the above would be *no*. You eat it because it tastes good and you like it.

Unfortunately most students develop relationships with the opposite sex, not to grow spiritually, not to develop their worldview, not to search for a lifetime mate. They do it because it feels good, it's fun, and they like it. Frankly, that answer isn't good enough in relationships. If you have that sort of approach to this whole issue, you'll wind up in situations that will be dictated by your drives and not by the standards that you set for yourself.

As one wise man once said, "Aim at nothing and you'll probably hit it." Take a few minutes now and write out a vision statement for your relationship life. _____

_____

_____

_____

_____

_____

_____

Take this vision statement and place it in your journal, on your calendar, on your bedroom door, or somewhere that will remind you of your purpose in developing relationships.

Relationships are all about choices. Read Zach's choice concerning his lifestyle and dating.

The first few years of high school, I was obsessed with the idea of finding a girlfriend. Everything I did seemed to revolve around dating and relationships. I was either depressed because I was not accepted by a girl, or I was on a relationship high because things were going well. It controlled my emotions, my thought life, my clothes, my money, my spare time, and just about everything else. It was like the lizard that ate New York! Then during my junior year, God really began to show me that I was trying to fill an emptiness that only He could fill. I never completely trusted God with my happiness. One night, after going through a painful break-up, God showed me this. It was like He was saying, "When are you going to stop trying and start trusting in Me?"

From now until the day I marry I am going to pray for my future wife, seek to be the man God wants me to be, and stop the meaningless hide-and-seek strategy of dating. I want to be available for God to fully use me; and I realize that if I am consumed in the dating game, I'll have very little energy for service and mission.

Personal Romance and Relationships True or False Test

___ **There is no physical, verbal, or emotional element in my relationships that would cause me shame after I marry God's girl for me.**

___ **There is no element of my relationships that would cause a girl shame or ill feelings later on after she marries.**

___ **My heart is pure concerning words, thoughts, and actions. I want the best for the girls I date, court, or with whom I share a friendship.**

___ **I am not dating a girl as an attempt to fulfill my drive for self-pleasure or for approval.**

___ **If I were to die today, it would be true that I tried to bless her spiritually and I didn't pressure her sexually.**

___ **I never talk with the guys in a demeaning way about the girls I date, court, or with whom I share a friendship. I speak the best of her.**

God has a purpose for our relationships. The example He sets is in His relationship with us. From the creation of man in *Genesis 2* to the beginnings of the early church and even into the discussion of the end times, the primary concern of God is whether or not humanity is in relationship with Him. When God first breathed life into man's nostrils, He set up for a relationship with Himself. As part of this relationship, He blessed humanity with life and instructions for living a joyful, abundant life. Our job is to be a blessing to those around us.

Read *Leviticus 19:18*.

What does it mean to love your neighbor as yourself? ____
_____
_____

Who is your neighbor? (See the story of the good Samaritan for help on this one. *Luke 10:25-37*) _____
_____
_____

There are many Scriptures about blessing others. It's not a question of whether we should decide to bless others or not. It is an instruction from God.

List as many ways you can think of to be a blessing to others. _____
_____
_____
_____
_____
_____

The Heart of the Matter–
Loving Others as Jesus Loves Us

Take the *1 Corinthians 13* Test. Answer yes or no.

1. **Are you patient with the growth and development of a relationship? Will you have Christlike love no matter how much waiting you encounter?** _____

2. Will you treat her with kindness, never mocking or belittling her? _____
3. Will you keep pride and boasting out of your relationships? _____
4. Will you refuse to grow bitter if a relationship ends? Are you willing to forgive and release a person if you are rejected? _____
5. Will you rejoice in truth? _____
6. Will you not revel in things that are evil? _____
7. Will you protect yourself and your relationships by following God's standard? _____
8. Will you give someone the same honor, blessing, and respect that God has given you? _____

What blessings are at the finish line for a righteous man?
❏ A powerful life story
❏ A healthy sexual relationship with your wife
❏ A purpose-driven lifestyle
❏ A tested ability to say no when tempted
❏ An understanding of God's faithfulness to provide outside of your striving to provide for yourself
❏ A testimony of achievement
❏ A heritage for your children
❏ A blessing upon your parents and grandparents

What possibilities await a man who didn't follow God's plan?
❏ Fear of Sexually Transmitted Diseases (venereal disease, AIDS, herpes)
❏ Inability to say no to infidelity in marriage
❏ Shame imputed upon you by Satan
❏ Feeling of dissatisfaction, constantly comparing your wife's sexual performance with that of other sexual partners
❏ An addictive lifestyle of sex
❏ Emotional scars

❑ An inhibition to talk to your kids about abstinence and purity
❑ Disrespect of those closest to you

Blessed is the man who does not walk in the counsel of the wicked or stand in the way of sinners or sit in the seat of mockers. But his delight is in the law of the Lord, and on his law he meditates day and night. He is like a tree planted by streams of water, which yields its fruit in season and whose leaf does not wither. Whatever he does prospers. Not so the wicked! They are like chaff that the wind blows away. Therefore the wicked will not stand in the judgment, nor sinners in the assembly of the righteous. For the Lord watches over the way of the righteous, but the way of the wicked will perish.
Psalm 1

To put this verse into the mix of what we've discussed, a righteous guy has a great future. The wicked have no future. It's as simple as that. So where do you go from here? We challenge you to make this decision:

Lord, I accept you as Lord over my entire life. I refuse to give in to the world's view of sex and dating. I make a commitment that my life will be an example of righteous living and holy integrity. I choose to honor women. I choose to uplift them, not tear them down. I choose to be a transformed, active, single-minded man who exemplifies Christian ethics in relationships. Thank you for granting me this opportunity. I want to make the most of these exciting and yet sometimes confusing years. You are all I need. I want nothing more; I will settle for nothing less.

Signed_____ **Date**_____